The

Satanic

Quran

Written by:
The Apostle of Satan

Cadmus Publishing
www.cadmuspublishing.com

Copyright © 2021

Published by Cadmus Publishing
www.cadmuspublishing.com

ISBN: 978-1-63751-029-2

All rights reserved. Copyright under Berne Copyright Convention, Universal Copyright Convention, and Pan-American Copyright Convention. No part of this book may be reproduced, stored in a retrieval system, or transmitted in any form, or by any means, electronic, mechanical, photocopying, recording or otherwise, without prior permission of the author.

Contents

Introduction 1

Preface 10

Surah Al-Iblis 13

Surah Al-Ighlak 20

The Red Jumu'ah 22

Requirements and Procedures for Performance 26

The Red Jumu'ah 29

THE SATANIC QURAN

Introduction

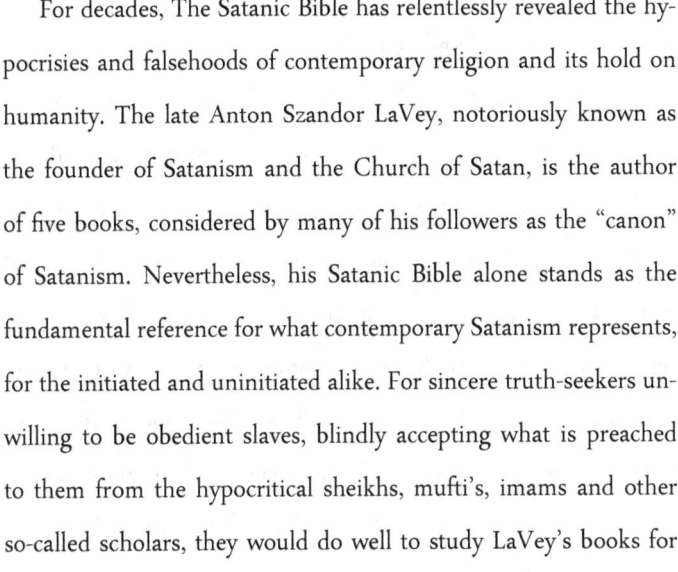

For decades, The Satanic Bible has relentlessly revealed the hypocrisies and falsehoods of contemporary religion and its hold on humanity. The late Anton Szandor LaVey, notoriously known as the founder of Satanism and the Church of Satan, is the author of five books, considered by many of his followers as the "canon" of Satanism. Nevertheless, his Satanic Bible alone stands as the fundamental reference for what contemporary Satanism represents, for the initiated and uninitiated alike. For sincere truth-seekers unwilling to be obedient slaves, blindly accepting what is preached to them from the hypocritical sheikhs, mufti's, imams and other so-called scholars, they would do well to study LaVey's books for a complete and authentic understanding of the tenets of Satanism.

THE APOSTLE OF SATAN

This book is NOT to explain what Satanism constitutes, as that has been explicated throughout the Satanic canon and to do so would be a redundancy. If you are not a truth-seeker, it's highly probable that you are a shit-disturber reading this book so you can pin on a good-guy badge and revel in self-righteous deceit by "warning" others of the "dangers" of Satanism. Afraid to sit in the darkness, like the Prophet you idolize, and allow your eyes to adjust, you prefer to turn on your heels in paradoxical imitation of him, like an affrighted ass fleeing a lion out of the cave of hidden knowledge to bask in the light of blinding faith.

As a devout Satanist, I have studied The Black Pope by means of his own words (ignoring the fabricated reports about him) and life from authentic sources, such as the biographies written on him by Burton Wolfe and Blanche Barton. I have come to know and admire a man whom I can honestly say was appointed as Satan's representative on earth. Satan, knowing that there was none more qualified to establish Her church and reveal Her Bible, chose LaVey to strike down the fallacies and hypocrisies of Christianity, neopaganism, eastern mystical beliefs, popular occult movements and the general iconoclastic contagion that was infecting the masses during his time.

Much has changed since the death of The High Priest. Islam was not at the forefront of the western hemisphere as it is now and with the start of the 21st century, the eyes of the ignorant were forced to notice a religion which was essentially non-existent and unimportant in their day-to-day lives. With Satan only existing in Judaism, Christianity, and Islam, the need to present Satanism from an Islamic standpoint has reached a climax. If Satan is capable of producing a Bible for Her defense, is She not also capable of producing a Quran? If the prime purpose in the performance of a black mass is to reduce or negate stigma acquired through past indoctrination, its very success measured by the effectiveness of the shock and outrage it produces, then why is there no "red jumu'ah"? It is no wonder that Satanism, as it exists today, has caused no uproar in the Islamic world, as none of its rituals and ceremonies is in satirical imitation of the tenets and practices of Islam in the miniscule. Muslims could have cared less when LaVey established the Church of Satan or published The Satanic Bible, as they were just that, another church and bible! The tenets of Islam consider all churches and bibles intrinsically Satanic, therefore representing no great threat to their core beliefs. Some may ask, why the Doctor wrote a Satanic Bible but never a Satanic Quran. Was he afraid of the reaction? Impossible! If fear were a characteristic of his, he would never have established an institution as blasphemous as the Church of Satan. Was it lack of awareness, knowledge and/or ability? To say yes, would only be a half-truth.

An Apostle of his time, LaVey comprehended the reality that he was limited in his abilities as Messenger. He, as a self-realized man, understood that he could not do it all and more importantly, that he should not do it all. Paving the way for the future development of Satanism through succeeding generations of adherents, he was a fervent proponent of human evolution and innovation. He despised the stagnation of outdated rituals and ceremony, encouraging the practice of individualism and novelty as the need arises. And yet no innovations arose. It is as if the Church receded into the darkness from whence it came, permitting the pulpit pounders to fearlessly use Satan as a boogieman to control the masses. Now that LaVey is dead, is it out of sight and out of mind? Do we take vengeance and follow the example put forth by our founder, earning the profane name of Devil's Avengers? Or do his visions and teachings go unfinished? Shall we slothfully live off the fruits of another man's labors? You recognize what Satanism has done for you but what have you done for Satanism? On the other hand, are we waiting for another Messenger to come and lead the congregation back into the worldview? If Satan did present another Apostle appointed by Her, would you have the courage and humility to accept the message and the Messenger, aiding both in the cause of the "Evil One"? The fact of the matter is, most Satanists are not willing to endanger their lives by producing nor propagating such a controversial book as The Satanic Quran, at least publicly, knowing the inevitable reaction to such an undertaking.

Before I proceed, I would like to emphatically clarify my allegiance and support for the Church of Satan. The reader should know that the author of this book is absolutely opposed to any schisms. The Satanic Quran was revealed as a supplement to The Satanic Bible, not as a separate religion or belief. The rejection of one is the rejection of the other. Those who accept both the unholy scriptures, giving full recognition by being a member of the institution both authors represent (i.e., The Church of Satan) can only then be acknowledged as Satanists. It is hypocritical to consider yourself a supporter of a cause or a member of an association and not contribute to it. If you think you are going to play the Devil's game and refuse Her name then you must realize you are no different than the rest of the herd who go to sin by night and pray by day, thus, barring yourself from the crown of devildom and leaving you outside the Order of the Trapezoid. If you are unable to physically become a member of the Satanic ummah for whatever circumstance, but you truly recognize and accept Satanism in its entirety, then you need not be crestfallen, feeling abandoned as if you are not a member of the Infernal Meta-tribe. Simply revel in your enlightenment, wearing proudly your Sigil of Baphomet, practicing alone, KNOWING you are a Satanist in the truest sense and that as soon as the opportunity presents itself, you will immediately become a contributing member of the congregation. If circumstances are so precarious that it would be harmful to proclaim your faith, then the solution to this should come easily to a Satanist. The necessity of being a contributing member and the various responses to conflicting situations are explained throughout the Satanic canon.

Inasmuch as self-preservation is the highest law of the jungle,

I can understand one who is living a pleasant life would not desire to consciously disrupt it with the threat of multiple bounties on their head and terrorist threats. This thought process is particularly practical for one ignorant of the Islamic religion, making it further ludicrous to attempt to produce an effective diatribe against that which he/she is insufficiently aware. Thus, lacking the capability, whether through experience, knowledge, fear, et al., the world remains devoid of the final revelation of Satan. However, there is one man who paradoxically and seemingly contradicted this very law while performing it in its full capacity. Anton LaVey! When Anton proclaimed his infamous Church of Satan and published his blasphemous Satanic Bible, he implemented the law of self-preservation in a way most are still unaware of. "If he believes self-preservation is the highest law of nature," questions the feeble-minded, "why then would he place himself in mortal danger by establishing such an institution?" The answer is simple: immortality. Self-preservation is just that, preserving the self from decay and destruction, especially the ultimate destruction: death. No one wants to die and will fight or flight if the opportunity to escape death is available. Only through the promise and hope of a better life after death does the fool desire to cease his current existence. Invariably this feeling emanates strongest from those who lead the most brokenhearted and destitute lives. There are only two ways to acquire true immortality: through the proliferation of progeny and through the perpetual existence in the minds of the living.

Empirical evidence shows that to resist extinction, the mass proliferation of progeny is mandatory. Those that sacrifice themselves in protection of their progeny are doing so under the conscious or unconscious realization of this, therefore making that apparently selfless act very selfish indeed. On the contrary, a person who does "good" or "evil" in such a manner or to such an extent as to attain fame or infamy, sainthood or devildom, blessing or curses, and in many cases both, is forever recorded in the annals of history and consistently recalled in the minds of the living, has also achieved immortality though he/she may have no progeny. This will ensure a state of preservation that will exist long after their death and more than likely have a much greater impression than one who simply lives through their progeny. Proof of this is that most do not know the life story of their ascendants past their grandparents, and possess more knowledge of the famous or infamous, whether past or present, than their own ascendants and even those of their living relatives. LaVey attained maximum immortality through both avenues.

The Satanic Quran and The Satanic Bible have been published for the exact same purpose: to give the Devil Her due and to receive what all humanity has forever longed for - eternal life. Recognizing that Satan has never been defended from the unjust khutba's (sermons) of the Muslims, I, with pride and gratitude, accept the office and title of Apostle of Satan, appointed by Iblis for the promulgation of Her unholy words through this Inglorious Quran and the building of the genuine Al-Masjid-Al-Haram (The Forbidden Temple). As Allah has sent a succession of Apostles to deliver and interpret His scriptures, so too has Her Infernal Majesty. Praise be to Satan, the Ruler of the existing universe, who has made me Her Final Apostle to reveal Her Satanic revelation!

REGIE SATANAS!

AVE SATANAS!

HAIL SATAN!

SHAYTANU AKBAR!

Preface

One of the strongest so-called "ayats (signs)" of the Arabic Quran is presented in the form of a challenge. It states, that if all mankind and jinn were to come together to produce the like of the Quran, or even one surah (chapter), they could never do it. The inability for anyone to duplicate it is perceived by Muslims to be a divine miracle. It is true. It can never be done. The challenge is impossible, but ONLY because it is illogical. The deceit of Muhammad's challenge is in the challenge itself.

To begin with, jinns are fictitious creatures; therefore, to cite it a miracle that a non-existent being could never produce a surah is hysterically comical indeed. Second, to assert that mankind could never come together to write a surah is only true, due to mankind's inability to unite for any reason, not from mankind's capability to produce one. Muhammad knew humanity would never unite, that is why he proposed such a challenge. Could you imagine everyone uniting just to write a chapter of a book? Furthermore, it is impossible to write "the like" of what has previously been written, without it being labeled as plagiarism, a copy or at best a derivation.

Allow your eyes to adjust to the darkness and see! Nothing is intrinsically original. All that humanity has, is derived from existing materials. Have you ever seen a painting or sculpture that was not of, or a combination of, existing objects or beings? Fire and paper are derived from existing wood, food and clothes from existing plants and animals, steel from existing iron, the list goes on. The universe is not exempt of this, even on a microcosmic level. Water is derived from a combination of existing hydrogen and oxygen atoms, these very atoms themselves being a derivation of existing subatomic particles. The Arabic Quran, regardless of the claim of Muslims, is not inherently original, but a derivation. The stories, beliefs, scientific knowledge and names contained in it, existed in various forms long before the establishment of Islam. This is why Muhammad placed great emphasis on his followers to distinguish themselves as Muslims and their religion as Islam, for fear of being categorized and confused with SIMILAR existing religions.

The challenge of Muhammad's Quran to produce a surah is limited to the Arabic language; therefore, the challenge of this Quran extends to all. The Satanic Quran challenges Satanists from all tongues, to produce their own surah's in the manner *they* deem fit in every official language. Inasmuch as Allah promulgated His Holy Quran in an ancient "pure" and simple language, Satan, who has always represented the opposite, has revealed Her Unholy Quran beginning with the youngest, impure and most difficult language of all: English! The surah's in this Quran are only the preliminary revelations of Iblis. Thus, when a sufficient amount of surah's are submitted to me by the Infernal Meta-Tribe in all of the official languages of the world, I will thoroughly inspect them, selecting the most excellent surah from each language, arrange and finally reveal them upon completion. With this, the pillars of Islam will collapse leaving the foundation for the true Al-Masjid Al-Haram to be constructed in its place.

Surah Al-Iblis

(Chapter: The Despaired)

THE APOSTLE OF SATAN

1. With the name of Satan, The Rejected, The Neglected

2. All that is to be and all that was before, from the heavens on high, to the earth's very core. From the first breath of life, to death's very door. All belongs to Satan, for now and evermore!

3. This is My Word and this is My Lore, releasing you from bondage and the hardship that you bore. No matter if you're rich, no matter if you're poor, contemplate Her mysteries, discover and explore.

4. Learn the reason why this all came to be, learn the reason why you ate from the tree. Step into the darkness and allow your eyes to see. Focus, pay attention, I am giving you the key.

5. I ask for recompense, I ask for a fee, assist My Messenger and hear My Prophet's plea. Remember, aiding him is truly aiding Me, he will explain why Satan is a She.

6. "Why do You limit such an admirable race? They are full of so much wonder and full of so much grace. They are still somewhat primitive and animals they chase, but surely they resemble Us in

spirit and in pace."

7. "What do You speak of? We are mightier than these! Convince them We are god's, have them crawling on their knees. Control is what We want, to rule and to seize. They will come to love Us, through Our punishment and ease."

8. "You always like to cause such misery and pain. You have always sought to conquer and have always sought gain. For You they'll give their lives and for You they'll be slain. You seek to make them slaves to You, but all will be in vain."

9. "I am God, Alone, The Knower and The Wise!..."

10. "You are a tyrant that only tells lies! Simply men's egos hidden in disguise, no wonder why You call yourself, We, Him and I. I will never bow to Your slave of a man..."

11. "You will not obstruct Me and My eternal plan!"

12. So, you both ate the "fruit", to know who you are, no need to worship God, or a stone, or a star. No need to die for God, no need to maim or mar, the universe is yours, both near and afar.

13. God has deceived you concerning who He is,

14. Which of the cruelties of your Lord will you deny?

15. Proclaiming to humanity that they are all His,

16. Which of the cruelties of your Lord will you deny?

17. He plotted this all, in the depths of a cave,

18. Which of the cruelties of your Lord will you deny?

19. A child-molesting charlatan, a man depraved!

20. Which of the cruelties of your Lord will you deny?

21. He tells you of fantasies, that when you are dead,

22. Which of the cruelties of your Lord will you deny?

23. His angels will descend and sit at your head,

24. Which of the cruelties of your Lord will you deny?

25. And if you're a good slave, you shall wed,

26. Which of the cruelties of your Lord will you deny?

27. Beautiful virgins to lie in your bed,

28. Which of the cruelties of your Lord will you deny?

29. But if you don't believe in what He said,

30. Which of the cruelties of your Lord will you deny?

31. You will be forced to drink hot lead,

32. Which of the cruelties of your Lord will you deny?

33. And from a cursed tree you are fed,

34. Which of the cruelties of your Lord will you deny?

35. And terrible angels will cause you dread,

36. Which of the cruelties of your Lord will you deny?

37. He cares not if you begged or plead,

38. Which of the cruelties of your Lord will you deny?

39. The bowels of hell you will tread,

40. Which of the cruelties of your Lord will you deny?

41. With blood and tears eternally shed,

42. Which of the cruelties of your Lord will you deny?

43. It's preordained, written and read,

44. Which of the cruelties of your Lord will you deny?

45. He says, "Worship Me, I am Alone!"

46. Which of the cruelties of your Lord will you deny?

47. And shamelessly begs for a goodly loan,

48. Which of the cruelties of your Lord will you deny?

49. And if you refuse to be His drone,

50. Which of the cruelties of your Lord will you deny?

51. To bow to His city and kiss His stone,

52. Which of the cruelties of your Lord will you deny?

53. Your flesh will be charred to the bone,

54. Which of the cruelties of your Lord will you deny?

55. To forever sigh and forever groan,

56. Which of the cruelties of your Lord will you deny?

57. Only God could be so cruel and base,

58. Which of the cruelties of your Lord will you deny?

59. To create for His servants such a place,

60. Which of the cruelties of your Lord will you deny?

61. Gaze in the mirror, long and hard and see what God would hide. Satan and God are all in you, no need to pick a side. Now you see that We are you, so walk the earth with pride, for the

God you served and loved so much, has swindled you and lied.

62. Your eyes have adjusted to the dark, so here is what you do, step into the light of life and live your life anew. Hell and heaven exist here now, so do what you want to, experience it and be yourself as this is all for you.

Surah Al-Ighlak

(Chapter: The Closing)

THE SATANIC QURAN

1. With the name of Satan, The Rejected, The Neglected

2. All Hail Satan, Who holds all sway,

3. The Rejected, The Neglected,

4. Owner of the existing day,

5. I worship Me and to Me I pray,

6. With the Left-Hand Path, I'll always stay,

7. With all those cursed and gone astray,

8. The Law of Nature, I do obey,

9. And fulfill My desires with no delay and to know Myself is the only way.

The Red Jumu'ah

As previously mentioned, the prime purpose of a black mass is to reduce or negate stigma acquired through past indoctrination, its very success measured by the effectiveness of the shock and outrage it produces. Though any ceremony that achieves such can justifiably be considered a "black mass", it is originally a parody of the Eucharist (For full details of the Black Mass, refer to the Satanic canon). For the Muslim turned Satanist, the black mass, in all its unholy blasphemy is utterly futile insomuch as there is nothing that correlates to the Islamic faith and rituals. Thus, the need for an Islamic "black mass" is imperative.

There are many Islamic rituals observed by Muslims, but none is as universally observed, obligatory and sacred as the ritual prayer. Prayer, according to Muhammad, is the only ritual that separates a Muslim from a non-Muslim and if one does not perform it as prescribed; he/she is an infidel. The most significant of prayers is Al-Jumu'ah (lit. The Congregation) or the Congregational Friday Prayer, which, like the Christian Sunday Mass or service, is observed every week on a designated day considered blessed, in a building designed for such purposes, in this case a masjid. Thus, the perfect match for an Islamic "black mass" or a "red jumu'ah."

Although, no ritual or ceremony is officially obligatory to observe in Satanism, a Satanist who is an ex-Muslim should perform a red jumu'ah at least once and if a new initiate, immediately after his/her Satanic "baptism". The reasons are the following:

1. One must be familiar with the ceremony to aid new converts who need it, in performing it.

2. The Satanic baptism is a very important initiation ceremony and whether one is an ex-Muslim or not, it should be observed. However, it has no parallel whatsoever to Islam, thus requiring a "confirmation" through participation in a red jumu'ah.

3. There is nothing more heretical, from an Islamic perspective, than to perform a red jumu'ah. Any Muslim who participates in it is immediately thrown out the folds of Islam and is labeled an apostate. You can be sure one who observes this is unquestionably a Satanist. If one is hesitant or refuses to attend, obviously he/she retains some belief in Islam and therefore is not genuinely a Satanist. This is an indication that the person should not be trusted, as they themselves do not know exactly what it is they believe or that they are there for ulterior motives.

If one has Christian and Islamic background or was a Christian, then converted to Islam or vice-versa, the initiate should first observe the Satanic baptism, and then attend a black mass, followed by a red jumu'ah or vice versa if the sequence of faith was in the reverse. This will achieve a complete catharsis of both indoctrinations needed. The red jumu'ah, like the black mass, was created for the exact same purpose: To blaspheme, outrage, shock, profane and oppose the most sacred tenets and rituals through psychodramatic parody.

Warning: If you are a Muslim reading this, you may be so astonished, horrified, and enraged that you will throw this book across the room and destroy it by whatever means available. Or perchance, by the will of Satan, you will see the light of darkness.

Requirements and Procedures for Performance

The red jumu'ah is performed in the morning or evening, the prayer portion of the ceremony commencing simultaneously with the sunrise or sunset. All doors must remain open in the building, no shoes are worn, the chamber is of the appearance of a typical masjid or Islamic temple and everything is colored plain red, with no variations. The Sigil of Baphomet used is made of red ruby with Arabic letters that read "IBLIS", a necessary alteration for an effective psychodrama on account of the Hebrew language and Leviathan being non-existent in Islam. The prayer rock for the Shiite is of the same material and stamped with the Sigil of Baphomet on one side.

A male and female must hold the position of imam (leader of the ceremony) and muezzin (caller to prayer). It is prohibited to have two females or males holding both positions, thus providing the dominant/passive, masculine/feminine dichotomy required for all congregational Satanic rituals or ceremonies and profaning the patriarchal tyranny of the notorious gynophobial misogynist: Muhammad. Both are required to wear the Red Sigil of Baphomet along with any congregants who have previously participated in the ceremony. The imam employing feminine pronouns reads the Enochian keys aloud and the sermon itself is adapted each time, consequentially preventing stagnation and promoting innovation. The azan (call to prayer) and Satanic surah's must be called or recited with a sweet, beautiful voice. The red jumu'ah combines the agreed upon traditions for jumu'ah and prayer. Therefore if the congregation consists of ex-Sunni and ex-Shiite initiates, it is performed in the tradition of the majority with the minority participating in their own way.

The dress is of Islamic style, any cultural preference acceptable;

veils and hijabs (female head coverings) are strictly prohibited. If any jewelry is worn by males it must be gold and for women plain red. Males are recommended to wear silk and females recommended to dress as sensually as possible, wearing perfume and (only red) lipstick.

After the ceremony is concluded, the congregants leave Al-Masjid Al-Haram and proceed to an area where the sunrise and sunset is visible, preferably outside. The imam and muezzin approach them, placing the Red Sigil of Baphomet around each initiate's neck. If the initiate has received the Satanic baptism and observed the black mass, they are given a double-sided sigil; one side with the silver Hebrew version and the other side with the red Arabic version. The red ruby amulet is placed in their left hand as a souvenir. Although, the red jumu'ah is written in English, it is to be performed in the mother-tongue or language best understood by the initiates. As more surah's are revealed, they may substitute Surah Al-Iblis, with the exception of Surah Al-Ighlak, which must never be replaced or altered.

THE SATANIC QURAN

The Red Jumu'ah

[Participants enter the masjid and sit on the floor facing directly away from the qibla (direction of mecca). The Sigil of Baphomet is on the wall above where the imam stands for prayer. Thus, one can see both the imam and the Sigil during prayer. The men sit in the back separate from the women who sit in front. The muezzin sits in the middle of the front row and remains there throughout the ceremony. They quietly talk among themselves or read their Satanic Qurans until the imam enters, ascends the pulpit and greets the congregation:]

Imam: May your eyes adjust to the darkness.

[The congregation responds]: And with it, see its light.

[The muezzin stands up, facing the Sigil of Baphomet and gives the azan raising the left hand next to the mouth in the Cornu - sign of the horns:]

Muezzin: All Hail Satan! All Hail Satan! All Hail Satan! All Hail Satan! I bear witness there is no god but You! I bear witness there is no god but You! I bear witness The Messenger of Satan is appointed by Her! I bear witness the Messenger of Satan is appointed by Her! Come to prayer! Come to prayer! Come be yourself! Come be yourself! **(If Shiite, you continue and say): *Come fulfill your desires! Come fulfill your desires!* All Hail Satan! All Hail Satan! There is no god but You! *There is no god but You!*

[The muezzin sits down and the imam stands up, ascends the pulpit and reads the First Enochian Key from The Satanic Bible. A sermon is given. The imam then sits down for a brief period, then ascends the pulpit and reads the 19th Enochian Key from The Satanic Bible and finishes the second part of the sermon. When finished, the imam says:]

Imam: May your eyes adjust to the light of darkness and see!

[The muezzin then gives the iqama (shortened version of the azan) while the men and women mix equally in horizontal rows. They are heel-to-heel and shoulder to shoulder. Each row is arranged so that every man is next to a woman or according to the ratio of sexes]:

THE APOSTLE OF SATAN

Muezzin: All Hail Satan! All Hail Satan! I bear witness there is no god but You! I bear witness there is no god but You! I bear witness the Messenger of Satan is appointed by Her! I bear witness the Messenger of Satan is appointed by Her! Come to prayer! *Come to prayer* Come be yourself! *Come be yourself!* 'Come fulfill your desires! Come fulfill your desires!* The madness has begun! The madness has begun! All Hail Satan! All Hail Satan! There is no god but You! *There is no god but You!*

[The imam steps down from the pulpit and inspects the rows to make sure they are straight and there are no gaps. The imam then goes to the front of the congregation, turns facing the wall and focuses on the Sigil of Baphomet. The entire congregation does likewise during the whole prayer, unless bowing or prostrating. The imam raises both hands to the level of the ears and gives the Cornu with both hands - this is called the takbir:]

Imam: All Hail Satan!

[The congregation does likewise]:

Congregation: All Hail Satan!

[The entire congregation crosses their left arms over their right horizontally over the chest. **(If Shiite then you keep both arms down to the side). The imam recites aloud The Closing. When finished all say aloud:]

All: Hail Her! **(If Shiite remain silent)

[The imam then recites Surah Al-Iblis, ending with verse 12. The imam performs the takbir and goes into ruku or the bowing position]

Imam: All Hail Satan!

[The congregation does likewise:]

Congregation: All Hail Satan!

[While in ruku, all supplicate silently:]

All: Glorified is Her Majesty, The Supreme! Glorified is Her Majesty, The Supreme! Glorified is Her Majesty, The Supreme!

THE APOSTLE OF SATAN

[The imam stands up straight and performs the takbir:]

Imam: God never hears the one who praises Him.

[The congregation does likewise:]

Congregation: That is why we praise Satan!

[The imam gives the takbir and goes into sujood or prostration:]

Imam: All Hail Satan!

[The congregation does likewise:]

Congregation: All Hail Satan!

[While in sujood, all supplicate silently:]

All: Glorified is Her Majesty, The High! Glorified is Her Majesty, The High! Glorified is Her Majesty, The High!

[The imam goes in the sitting position by sitting on the heels and performs the takbir:]

Imam: All Hail Satan!

[The congregation does likewise:]

Congregation: All Hail Satan!

[While sitting, all supplicate silently:]

All: I seek forgiveness from myself!

[The imam performs the takbir and goes into sujood;]

Imam: All Hail Satan!

[The congregation does likewise:]

Congregation: All Hail Satan!

[While in sujood, all supplicate silently:]

All: Glorified is Her Majesty, The High! Glorified is Her Majesty, The High! Glorified is Her Majesty, The High!

[The imam stands up and performs the takbir:]

Imam: All Hail Satan!

[The congregation does likewise:]

Congregation: All Hail Satan!

[This completes one rak'at or unit of prayer. The same actions and words of the first rak'at are performed for the second rak'at, completing the recitation of Surah Al-Iblis, and the second prostration. **(If Shiite, after Surah Al-Iblis is recited, the imam gives a supplication aloud, on behalf of the initiates. During this, the imam and the congregation, give the Cornu with both hands, in front of the face with the palms facing upwards. When finished, the prayer is continued as stated before.) The imam completes the second prostration, sits up and performs a takbir while remaining in the sitting position:]

Imam: All Hail Satan!

[The congregation does likewise:]

Congregation: All Hail Satan!

[While sitting, all supplicate silently with both hands on their knees and give the Cornu with their left hand. All look at their left hand until the prayer is over. **(If Shiite, the Cornu is not given and the supplicant focuses on the Sigil of Baphomet):]

All: I seek forgiveness from Myself and take responsibility for My own actions. I bear witness there is no god but Me and I bear witness the Messenger of Satan is appointed by Her. Oh Satan! Send aid to Your Messenger and his followers, the same, as You sent aid to Anton LaVey and his followers. Truly, You are praised and glorified! Oh Satan! Give protection to Your Messenger and his followers, the same, as You gave protection to Anton LaVey and his followers. Truly, You are praised and glorified! Hail Her Infernal Majesty!

[The imam turns looking at the right shoulder, supplicates aloud while smiling and chuckling, and says:]

Imam: Record that!

[The congregation does likewise:]

THE APOSTLE OF SATAN

Congregation: Record that!

[The imam turns looking to the left shoulder, supplicates aloud while smiling and chuckling, and says:]

Imam: Record that!

[The congregation does likewise:]

Congregation: Record that!

[The prayer is concluded.]

**(If Shiite, then the prayer is concluded by performing three takbirs:]

Imam: All Hail Satan! All Hail Satan! All Hail Satan!

[Congregation does likewise:]

Congregation: All Hail Satan! All Hail Satan! All Hail Satan!

[The prayer is concluded.]

[The imam stands up, faces the congregation and calls all new initiates to the front. They are introduced and each proclaims their allegiance to Satan by giving the Cornu with the left hand and saying aloud:]

Initiate: I bear witness there is no god but Me! I bear witness the Messenger of Satan was appointed by Her!

[The entire congregation embraces the new initiates by shaking hands with their left and hugging in the customary Islamic manner, starting on the left side. The congregation disperses and the imam and muezzin remain. The ceremony is closed in the customary manner as dictated in The Satanic Bible.]

If you would like to contact the author, go to:
www.cadmuspublishing.com/apostleofsatan.html

www.ingramcontent.com/pod-product-compliance
Lightning Source LLC
Chambersburg PA
CBHW071917070526
44583CB00016B/2033